Handbook
FOR
Church
Secretaries

Handbook
FOR
Church
Secretaries

E. Jane Mall

Abingdon
Nashville

HANDBOOK FOR CHURCH SECRETARIES

Copyright © 1978 by Abingdon

Library of Congress Cataloging in Publication Data

MALL, E JANE, 1920-
   Handbook for church secretaries.
   Includes index.
   1. Church secretaries—Handbooks, manuals, etc. I. Title.
   BV705.M34   651'.371   78-17213

ISBN 0-687-16565-2

Scripture quotations are from *The Living Bible* copyright © 1971 Tyndale House Publishers, Wheaton, Illinois. Used by permission.

MANUFACTURED BY THE PARTHENON PRESS AT NASHVILLE, TENNESSEE, UNITED STATES OF AMERICA

PREFACE

As an author, I'm constantly searching for things to write about. I'm also aware of the rule that says, "Write about those things you know best."

Still, I worked as a church secretary for five years and, even though my boss was always saying, "Jane, you must write a book about church secretaries!" I didn't pay any attention to that idea.

Then one day, in a church publication, I read a letter from a church secretary asking if there was any book published for church secretaries, one to help them on the job; the answer was no, nothing available, so I got busy.

The *Handbook for Church Secretaries* is the result, and I hope that it is a truly helpful book to a lot of church secretaries.

However, I can't take all the credit for this book because I didn't write it all by myself, and there are a few people who must be thanked.

My boss, the Reverend David Bebb Jones, who encouraged me to write the book, and who always gave me free reign when I'd get an idea for a new way to do a job, or when I'd come up with a new form or procedure. All church secretaries should be blessed with a boss like that!

Janet Andersen, a dear friend, who was not a church secretary but knew as much about the job as I did. "Andy" was always helpful and always had creative ideas.

My pastor, the Reverend K. K. Engel, and his secretary, Anita Goss, who read parts of my manuscript and contributed some invaluable suggestions. In our church we couldn't possibly get along without Anita, and I am so fortunate in having a pastor who is, in every way, most loving and supportive.

Marge Nickoley and Maxine Speyer are volunteer church secretaries who give of their time and talents on a regular basis and offered their views of a church secretary's job from a different perspective. They are loving, generous people.

Mae Schwarz, who works in a large church, gave me the benefit of her experiences, which helped me a lot in putting this book together.

And last but not least, my friend David

Enna who edited the manuscript. Dave works full time as an editor, so working with me meant giving up many evening and weekend hours. He corrected my punctuation and spelling errors, but he did much more than that. No trite word or sloppy phrase got past him; no involved title was allowed to stay when a simpler one would do. He questioned everything I wrote and asked questions and demanded answers. I'd deliver a neatly typed manuscript section to him, and get it back so red-penciled I could have cried. But I went to work, and we have a much better book because of Dave's interest and talent.

One more thing, throughout the book I have referred to church secretaries as she and to pastors as he. I realize, of course, that there are female pastors and male church secretaries, but in the interest of readability we have referred to church secretaries as she and pastors as he. To continually have to read he/she becomes quite tiresome! I hope that all women pastors and male church secretaries will understand.

E. Jane Mall

CONTENTS

*For God is not unfair. How
can he forget your hard work
for him, or forget the way you
used to show your love for him—
and still do—by helping his
children? And we are anxious that
you keep right on loving others
as long as life lasts, so that
you will get your full reward.*
                        (Hebrews 6:10)

*Work hard so God can say to
you, "Well done." Be a good
workman, one who does not need
to be ashamed when God examines
your work.*

                        (II Timothy 2:15a)

*Don't refuse to accept
criticism; get all the
help you can.*

                        (Proverbs 23:12)

*He says to you: I know
how many good things
you are doing. I have
watched your hard work
and patience.*

                        (Revelation 2:2a)

INTRODUCTION

This book was written for the church secretary on the job. It was written to help her and to stimulate her to do a better, more creative job. However, a few words directed to those who would like to be church secretaries is in order.

I had worked as a church secretary for five years when circumstances made it necessary for me to resign. The pastor placed an ad for a church secretary in the local newspapers and asked me to interview the applicants before setting up an appointment for him to talk to them.

It would seem that all secretaries know that on a job interview you should look neat and well groomed, and that you should feel relaxed about your appearance. These are pretty basic rules, but I was amazed and surprised when I started interviewing the applicants. One girl came in wearing blue jeans, with long straggly hair, and she was quite actively chewing on a wad of gum.

Another, when asked to take a typing test, said "Oh no, I'm not a very good typist!" But she wanted to be a church secretary.

Being a church secretary is an important, fascinating job, and it must be taken seriously. It requires many skills and a certain type of personality.

During your initial interview, the subject of salary will, of course, arise. You know what you're worth, what you can make in other secretarial jobs, and what you need to live on. The pastor knows what his council (or board of deacons or whatever it's called) has told him the church will pay a secretary. If you're lucky it comes out the same.

But if it doesn't, don't make the mistake of saying, "Well, I'll be working and making money, and I'll be serving the church too." If you want to serve your church, do it in your own church. Do all the volunteer work you can handle. What you do in the church where you are employed is a job, and you'll be paid a salary to do that job. So if the salary offered to you is inadequate, don't be afraid to negotiate. The pastor will probably have to go again to his council, but hang in there. Be fair, be honest, but don't take peanuts because you'll be "doing something for the church." That's actually demeaning the position of church secretary, and the job is a very important one and worthy of a decent salary. No matter what your salary, you'll earn it.

There are some church secretaries who work in the church where they are members, and for them it works out very well. Still, the same rules concerning salary and the general approach to the job remain the same.

Make sure that the minister outlines your duties and work hours. Ask him if you'll be expected to attend meetings, time in addition to your regular nine to five hours. If he says yes, ask about compensation for those hours (money or time off). Be businesslike. Know what you're getting into. After all, what you're saying is, "I'll be a good church secretary. I'll devote my time and my effort to doing the best job I can, and I expect to be compensated properly for the job I do." If that isn't appreciated, and the church still wants a full-time secretary for as little as possible, go elsewhere. This land is filled with churches, and most would welcome you with open arms and a decent salary. I know a few church secretaries who play the martyr and drag themselves to the church office on Saturdays and in the evenings, who are practically at the beck and call of the pastor and the congregation, and in no case is it a happy situation.

The thing is, churches usually aren't run like a business. Most pastors are not business administrators. The church's work is all of life to the pastor, and he thinks nothing of working at his job from 8 A.M. on through the last committee meeting that adjourns at midnight. You can't do this. The next morning the pastor may sleep late, but you have to be at your desk. So if you will be expected to attend meetings outside of your regular working hours, make arrangements at the start for some kind of compensation agreeable to you and to the pastor.

Now you've got the job and you come to work on Monday morning. You may have your predecessor training you for a week or two; you may not. Eventually, you'll find that you need a system to organize your work. If you've worked as a secretary in a business office where you've been told what to do and how to do it, your first weeks as a church secretary will blow your mind. You can be quite creative, and it will be appreciated. You probably won't run into the situation nearly all secretaries encounter on a new job: "You may have done it that way at your last job, but we do it differently here." On one job I was told: "Please! No creative typing. Just type!" As a church secretary you are more or less able to decide for yourself how to do your job.

If you're already working as a church secretary, it is my hope that some of the ideas and suggestions in this book will help to make your job more effective and more exciting. As you know, we church secretaries don't usually come to a working situation with well-planned office procedures, printed forms, and rules and regulations to follow. "We've been doing it this way" or "The last church secretary did it that way" is what we're told, and then it's up to us to continue in the same way or to devise our own way of working. During my years as a church secretary I had a lot of fun making up forms, trying new ways of doing certain jobs, learning to meet the challenge of doing a job efficiently with as little money as possible, and in learning how to deal with a lot of different people.

How many times I longed for a book or manual that would direct me and help me to do a better job. This book is a result of those longings. I began to write this book with the assumption that the reader is a secretary (church or another kind), and that she is a fast, accurate typist, knows shorthand and/or dictaphone, can manage at least a minimum of simple bookkeeping chores, knows how to answer the phone and to file. So this book deals with the specialties of the church secretary's job, the many things a church secretary is called on to do which she would probably never have to do in a business office. I've tried to explain these specialties, how to do them, and, in many instances, how to be creative and make something very special of these tasks. Just for fun, I started making a list of all the things a church secretary does on the job, and the list goes on and on and on. So, if I've left something out of this handbook, it's understandable. However, I've tried my best to include the more important aspects of the church secretary's job.

WHAT IS A CHURCH SECRETARY?

A secretary usually works for one person, and she is hired to relieve a busy person of the details of office work.

A church secretary is so much more than that! She is hired to do the office work that a minister would ordinarily have to do himself. Otherwise, he would have to rely on volunteers to help him, and since much of his work is of a confidential nature and his volunteers are members of his congregation, the minister without a church secretary winds up doing a lot of the routine work himself.

However, he needs much more than a person who is a good typist and knows how to file and answer the phone. The minister needs a person who is friendly, who genuinely likes people, and who can overlook his frailties. The church secretary has more than one boss (if she works for a congregation of 1,500 souls, she has 1,501 bosses), and she has to have a lot of composure.

The minister needs someone who is able to hear and know many confidential things about many people and keep them all to herself, and never take sides.

The pastor needs someone who is a self-starter and who can put plans and ideas into action on her own. When he is attending a meeting, counseling, or conducting a funeral or wedding, the minister needs the assurance that the church secretary is able to carry on alone.

It goes without saying that a church secretary is reliable and honest and a hard worker. These are traits desired in any good secretary. Besides that, it is essential that the church secretary be pleasant in her dealings with the congregation, be discreet in her dealings with the general public, and be adamant about relieving the minister of as much of the everyday workload as possible.

In conclusion, as a church secretary you will discover that you are thought of in different ways, by different people. If you're an efficient church secretary this won't faze you at all. Following are some of the ways different people view the church secretary.

The Church Secretary Viewed by the Minister

The minister is your boss and views the church secretary in many ways. First, he looks to you as the person who will get the paper and office work of the church done efficiently and on time. He expects you to be a hard worker and a self-starter.

He sees you as a keeper of secrets. In your position you will see and hear confidential things, and he depends on you to keep them to yourself, to refrain from offering your feelings about them, and to refuse to be caught in the middle of arguments or controversies.

The minister sees you as a liaison between himself and the congregation, and between himself and the general public. How you handle this is extremely important.

He sees you as a person who is loyal to him. When members of the congregation talk about the minister he is secure in the knowledge *Most Important* that you are letting it all flow in one ear and out the other, without comment.

The Church Secretary Viewed by the Congregation

The members of the congregation are also your boss. They are paying your salary. They make many demands on your time; they take up your time talking; they often expect the impossible of you. Some are considerate, others not so considerate. Some treat you as a friend, some as an employee. No matter, they'll all like it just fine if you're organized and efficient, if you smile, offer them a cup of coffee and keep on working!

The Church Secretary Viewed by the Church Secretary

A nine to five job. A complicated job and one which requires many skills and talents. A job that requires beyond the usual secretarial skills, a love for people, a special loyalty to the boss, and an understanding of the church and how it works. Also, an opportunity, as in few other jobs, to be creative and to derive an enormous amount of satisfaction and sense of achievement.

THE VOLUNTEER CHURCH SECRETARY

In the church we hear about the call. A minister was called by God, a person feels called to serve on a committee or to do some special work in the church.

Although a church secretary may consider herself called to her job, she should also realize that it is a job. A job is a job is a job. All church secretaries should repeat this daily. Although a paid secretary may rightly consider herself as called to her job, she must also realize that this is a job, a way of making a living. She can answer her call to God and her church in many other ways. How a church secretary feels about her job is a personal matter, of course.

The volunteer church secretary is something different. Surely, to volunteer to do this job for her church, with no pay, must involve a call.

The volunteer church secretary probably does not work from nine to five, five days a week. In all probability, she works when needed, or maybe puts in a scheduled two-to-three days a week, or just performs certain duties regularly. There may even be a team of volunteer church secretaries. I know of a church where there are four volunteers. They're called the Monday secretary, the Tuesday secretary, and so on. Each has a well-defined job that she performs on her day. They have devised an efficient method of leaving notes, which works very well for all. It doesn't matter how it's arranged, the important thing is that the work is accomplished.

25

The salaried church secretary wants to do the best possible job, just as she would in any other secretarial job. She wants to become as proficient as she can and be as much help to the minister and congregation as she can. That's what she's being paid for. The volunteer church secretary should be as dedicated and determined to be efficient because she has admitted to answering a call for God to perform this service for His church.

Let's say you're a volunteer church secretary, and, after reading this book, have some ideas on improving the system in your church. However, initiating these ideas and putting them into action will take a lot of time, and you are not in a position to give this much time. Still, you'd like to see these things done, and you know that the minister and the congregation would be appreciative. Why not organize a volunteer committee to accomplish the things you think are needed?

First, determine what you'd like to see accomplished. Make a list, jot down why you think these things should be initiated. You may, for example, see a real need in your church for a monthly newsletter or for a more efficient way of maintaining the church membership list.

After you have the minister's okay, work on getting as many people as you'll need.

Explain what you hope to accomplish and why. Talk about your call and what it means to you. Explain that if they feel called to this service you will welcome them as coworkers.

Once you have this committee (which you have carefully selected by individual skills and talents), call a meeting. Using this book as a guide, along with your own ideas and the pastor's, describe the jobs to be done. Let the committee members decide which jobs they want to tackle, and then, as a committee, determine how and when to get started.

It probably won't be easy to find many people who believe as you do that they are called to serve their church, but if you're fortunate enough to find them, a lot of work will be done, and all of you will derive a great satisfaction. And the church will benefit.

THE CHURCH SECRETARY'S OFFICE

A business office is a business office. Some have beautiful furniture, carpeted floors, and are luxurious, pleasant places in which to work. Some are dusty, uncomfortable, and noisy. Most are somewhere in between.

Church secretaries' offices also vary widely. Some share an office with the pastor, some have their own offices, and some occupy a desk in a corner of the church office. No matter what it's like, it's probably where you spend the better part of your waking hours, and it's the place many people associate with you. Naturally, you want to make it as attractive and efficient a working area as possible.

If you're one of the few church secretaries with a lovely, big desk, colored phone, carpeted floor, lots of file cabinets, and a bright red typewriter, you may not be interested in this chapter. The rest of you (I suspect the majority) read on.

If you share an office with the pastor, try to get a place of your own. This is a poor arrangement for both the minister and church secretary. Let's face it, part of your job is to take away some of the clergyman's burden of distractions. Your phone is ringing, your typewriter is clicking away, you're talking to custodians, members of the congregation, and tradespeople. How does the minister manage to concentrate? And what about when a couple comes to the minister with marital problems. What do you do? Leave your work until he's finished? Or does he have to take the couple to his home or the church basement where they will probably be interrupted? Unless there is absolutely no way of changing the arrangement, something should be done. At the very least, a wall or partition could be constructed between the minister's desk and yours.

If you occupy a desk in the church office along with the files, the mimeograph and ditto machines, and church library books, you can still create your own office. Do it with screens, room dividers, even the file cases. Make it your own, with plants, pictures, posters. If it's a very large church office and if the pastor approves, you could get someone to make two rooms of it, with a door leading from your office to the room where the office machines and files are kept.

However you manage it, try to have an attractive, efficient office. Try also, if at all possible, to arrange for your work area to be locked when you're not there. How many of us return to our desks on Monday morning to find the desk drawers in a complete mess, pens, and pencils gone, papers (and worse) scattered all over the desk, our typewriter keys jammed? There is no excuse for this, and it's up to you to insist on a work area that's strictly yours.

Important

29

Explain to the minister that it's important that you have an office or work area or desk that's strictly yours, to be locked when you're out of the office. Surely he will understand and will help you, as much as he possibly can, to get what you'd like.

Once you have your office the way you want it, keep it neat and attractive. In time, the people of the congregation will respect your rights. If they are used to considering that desk or office their own whenever you're not there, it will probably take some time, but keep at it.

THE STAFF AND STAFF MEETINGS

Depending on the size of the church and its budget, the staff will vary. It may consist of the pastor and the church secretary and a part-time custodian, or the staff may consist of many people.

In any case, the staff is divided into two classifications: professional and nonprofessional. A large staff could consist of one or more of the following categories, with one or more persons in each.

PROFESSIONAL

> Minister
> Assistant minister
> Associate minister
> Minister/Director of Christian Education (DCE)
> Administrative Assistant
> Youth Minister
> Minister of Music

NONPROFESSIONAL

> Church secretary
> Pastor's secretary
> Educational secretary
> Financial secretary
> Receptionist
> Typist
> Custodian

Regardless of the size of the staff, there should be a personnel committee composed of members of the congregation. This committee should be chosen carefully (ideally, it should be made up of persons who work in personnel) and each member's duties should be outlined. The committee should interview, hire, and fire. Members should be available to every staff member on request.

The church staff should have regularly scheduled staff meetings. These can be held for one-half hour once a month, two hours every Monday, or anywhere in between. If the staff is large and the amount of work varies, meetings are probably necessary at least once a week. But even if it's only the pastor, church secretary, and custodian, the staff should meet regularly.

Type and reproduce an agenda for every staff meeting. Staff members are to give you items for the agenda. The DCE may want to announce a special mailing to all students in the church school; the custodian may have a need to talk about his workload; the minister may have directions and guidance for all. Everyone on the staff should be allowed the opportunity to share his concerns, It is important, however, to stick to the agenda and to the time allotted for the meeting. Staff members must realize that if they don't get an agenda item to you on or before the deadline, it is likely to be discussed last, and then only if time permits. Thus, you should have no problems with deadlines. Some items—such as a request for a raise—would not be discussed at staff meetings. These would be taken to the personnel committee.

Staff meetings should be informal. Perhaps you could provide coffee or a soft drink. It might be a good idea to meet at lunch, either at a restaurant or with everyone bringing a sack lunch. However you do it, make sure that the atmosphere is relaxed and informal.

Let the congregation know the day and time of the staff meetings and request that they not call at that period. However, you may have to secure the services of a volunteer to answer the phone during the staff meeting.

The church secretary should make an effort to see that the meetings start and end on time. You are not the chairperson, the minister is, but the schedule should be your responsibility. I'm not advocating a gavel or alarm clock, perhaps just a gentle reminder to the minister, but keep your eye on the clock.

PUBLIC RELATIONS

What is this thing called public relations, and how is the church secretary concerned with it? Public relations is another way of saying communicating: It's something we do constantly, but do we do it effectively? How can we help others, ourselves, our friends to communicate more effectively?

Someone calls the church office and asks

the church secretary when a certain meeting is to be held. The church secretary answers, "I really don't know. No one has told me." The caller asks to speak to the pastor and the church secretary responds by saying that he is out and she doesn't know when he'll be back. The caller hangs up.

This is an example of poor public relations.

Another church secretary receives a call similar to the one in the above example. Her reply is, "I don't know when this meeting is scheduled, but I'm sure our minister knows. He's out of the office at the moment, but as soon as he returns, I'll ask him for that date and I'll call you."

Now, that's good public relations. That church secretary is open to the needs of another person and responds with an offer to help. (By the way, she should hardly ever have to say that she doesn't know when the minister will return to the office. An efficient church secretary asks her boss when he expects to return.)

Church secretaries, who do a lot of communiating in many different ways, should concern themselves with public relations and take a good long look at how they are handling this important aspect of their jobs and how they can make improvements.

Most clergymen are very concerned with

public relations—the way in which they communicate with the members of the congregation, with prospective members, with the general public, and with sister congregations. The minister knows it is an important part of his job. Some may handle this aspect of their ministry easily and naturally. For others, it is a constant struggle, a part of their job with which they are not entirely comfortable. For a few, it may even be a job which is completely beyond them. A clergyman may be an excellent preacher, organizer, and teacher, but just not able to do very much about the actual mechanics of public relations. Of course, through his preaching and teaching, he's involved in public relations, but his communications may be limited.

The clergyman you work for will be one of the above, and any of them will appreciate a church secretary who is aware of the importance of public relations. This is a very important part of the church's ministry and must be planned, effective, and productive. A church secretary is especially valuable if she knows something about the mechanics of creative communicating.

To some, the words "public relations" have a negative connotation. But what we're really talking about is communicating with people, specifically with the members of the church, with persons who may become members, with people who belong to other churches, with the professional staffs of sister churches, and with the general public. How can we effectively communicate with all of these people? It need not take years of training. The church secretary has many devices available to her, including:

the Sunday bulletin
news releases to local papers, radio, and TV
the church newsletter
the telephone
personal contacts
meetings
letters
special mailings

Take your list of ways to communicate. Write them down, one by one, perhaps a page for each one, and then over the next weeks and months jot down ways in which these methods could be improved. Ideas will come to you, you'll get ideas from other publications, and things will be brought to your attention that will serve as springboard ideas.

The Sunday Bulletin

The Sunday bulletin is mainly a means of communicating with the people (members and visitors) who attend worship services. But how can you extend this means of communication? Do you find yourself throwing away a lot of leftover bulletins on Monday morning? Why not mail these to absentee members, to people who are ill or in the hospital, to people who visited once or twice and haven't returned in several weeks.

The Church Newsletter

The church newsletter is a way for the pastor to communicate to the members of the congregation and for the members to communicate with each other.

Avoid boredom. Don't put out the same newsletter each week or month, with nothing different about it except the words. Constantly explore new forms, different ways of expressing a thought.

Make a list of sister congregations in the

community and send them a copy of your newsletter along with a letter explaining that you have put them on your regular mailing list and that you would appreciate receiving their newsletters. Read their mailings as carefully as you read your own. Do they contain techniques or ideas that could improve your newsletter? Such exchanges could stimulate a sense of competition, and would certainly be an excellent way of exchanging ideas.

News Releases

News releases to local newspapers allow the pastor and the congregation to communicate with the general public. This general public includes members of your and other churches, people who couldn't care less about any church, and people who will perhaps eventually join a church.

Be sure to establish some sort of personal relationship with the editor who decides which news items are published. Call in person, find out how the news releases are to be submitted, what the deadlines are, what your reasonable expectations can be. Remember what you're told and strictly adhere to the directions. If they ask that all items be double-spaced on one side of the paper and in before Thursday at 10 A.M., do it.

Think carefully through the items you submit. Consider the audience. Would the general public be interested in hearing about a rummage sale or a spaghetti dinner which are open to the public? Probably. Would they care that Mrs. Jones of the congregation is going to lead a Bible study in her home on Wednesday morning? Probably not. The editor will appreciate it if you weed out the not-so-newsworthy items.

The Telephone

The telephone, as annoying an instrument as has ever been invented—particularly for a church secretary—is still of vital importance. On many days, the telephone provides our only personal contact with people. How we use this instrument is important. It is an effective tool to use in public relations. The minister for the most part doesn't answer the phone. That's your job as church secretary, and you will handle many of the calls without bothering him at all.

No Problem

You're concentrating on typing the Sunday

39

bulletin, or putting together the annual report, or writing a news item. The phone rings every few minutes. By the time you've picked up that phone five or six times your patience is wearing thin, understandably so. Still, you must regard the phone as one of your best tools for public relations. Answer pleasantly. "Good morning, Grace Church. May I help you?" sounds good. That person has called the church only once this week, and he is not aware that you have answered the phone many times this morning. This is his personal contact with someone (you) who represents this particular church. See every phone call as an excellent means toward good public relations.

Personal Contact

Personal contact is another means of effective public relations. A lot of people come into the church office and talk to the church secretary. The list is endless and includes committee chairpersons with items for the newsletter, church school teachers with things to be dittoed, board members with minutes to be typed and distributed, people wanting to talk to the minister, volunteers offering their services, trades people, sales people, people wanting to use the church.

If you're busy and rushed and you're curt with a salesman, he probably isn't going to talk about *you.* He's going to talk to others about "that church. Very unfriendly sort of place." And you've blown a chance for good public relations.

Keep your office or work area as neat and attractive as possible. You could offer coffee to someone who has to wait. You might have some religious or general interest publications on a table. You might have a radio, turned low, so that soft music provides a pleasant background (nice for you, too).

Meetings

Meetings are the lifeblood of the congregation. There is no other way for the members of a committee, board, or organization to get together and discuss, make decisions, and formulate plans. So what does the church secretary, in the role of public relations, have to do with meetings? Quite a bit. It begins with a committee chairperson calling to see if the committee can meet in a certain room on a specific day and at a specific time.

41

You could check your calendar, say yes, jot that committee's name on the calendar for that date and forget it. And in so doing, you'd blow another opportunity for good public relations. It is much better to follow through, find out how many people will be attending the meeting and arrange with the custodian to be sure there are enough chairs and tables. Consider what is needed at a meeting. Will they need a chalkboard? Will they be serving refreshments? You can get others to do the actual work, but you should see to it that the meeting room is arranged appropriately. A helpful tool could be a room set-up form. This form can allow you to get all the needed details quickly and accurately.

If you and the minister have agreed that you will attend meetings to take notes or minutes, consider it an excellent opportunity for public relations. Be in command of the situation in an interested, cooperative way. Be a hostess, but also be an organizer. Then, you've doubled your value.

Letters

Letters are a common form of communicating. Of course, letters should be neatly typed, free of errors, and follow a regular business form. Most letters will be dictated by the minister, but you will write some, too. You will have to communicate with tradespeople about supplies, about errors in billings. You may write letters explaining that the minister is away at a convention or on vacation and that you will bring a certain matter to his attention upon his return. You may write letters to former members requesting information. In fact, you will probably compose and type and sign a good many letters (if you are not already, you should be). Look and discover how much correspondence you can handle for your boss.

Special Mailings

Special mailings are another effective way of communicating, and you can be a big help in making them as effective as possible. Usually, these are sent out to draw particular attention to an event or program that the minister feels deserves special publicity.

Keep a file copy of every special mailing you send out, and review it often. Are you becoming hooked on one technique? What was bad or good about some of them? Why?

How can they be improved? (If you're on the mailing list of sister congregations, you'll receive their special mailings and can glean ideas from them.)

As you can see, public relations, the act of communicating, is very important. You're looking for ways to elevate the position of church secretary, to make it an admired and respected profession, and there are many opportunities to do this through the art of communicating. Keep records, think creatively about what you've done, what you are doing, and what you hope to do. Come up with ideas, and be helpful and innovative.

Sample news release

SPAGHETTI DINNER
November 2, 1978
Jane Smith 555-1793

FOR IMMEDIATE RELEASE
The members of Grace Church, 101 Main Street, Lombard, will serve a Spaghetti Dinner at the church on November 28, from 5 to 9 P.M.

The public is cordially invited. The menu includes spaghetti, with a delicious homemade sauce, garlic bread, tossed salad, tea or milk, and homemade pie or cake. The cost is $2.50 per adult and $2 for children under six.

For further information, contact:
Jane Smith 555-1793
Grace Church
101 Main Street

Room Set-up Form

Fellowship Hall

```
┌─────────────────────────────────────┐
│                                      │
│              STAGE                   │
│                                      │
├─────────────────────────────────────┤
│                                      │
│                                      │
│                                      │
│                                      │
│                                      │
│                                      │
│                          ┌──────┐    │
│                          │ DOOR │    │
└──────────────────────────┴──────┴────┘
```

We have the following items on hand. Please check those you will need and indicate where you want them placed:

name of committee:_____
date of meeting:_____
time of meeting:_____
no. of people expected:____

chalkboard___ lectern___   /s/_____
tables___ chairs___
overhead projector___
Will you be serving refreshments? yes___   no ___
If yes, will you need to use the kitchen and equipment?

45

Room Set-up Form

CLASSROOM NO. 6

We have the following items on hand. Please check those you will need and indicate where you want them placed:

name of committee: *Bible Study Group*
date of meeting: *6/10/78*
time of meeting: *10:00 AM.*
no. of people expected: *50*
/s/ John Jones, chairman

chalkboard___ lectern _x_
tables _X_ chairs _x_
overhead projector ___
Will you be serving refreshments: yes _X_ no___.
If yes, will you need to use the kitchen and equipment? *No*

WORKING WITH VOLUNTEERS

As a church secretary you will deal with volunteers, as in very few other secretarial jobs. These are people who offer to help whenever and wherever they can. Because you are dealing with all types of people, this part of your job can be one of the most enjoyable, and at the same time, one of the most aggravating. It has been said that working with volunteers requires a special skill, and no doubt that is true, but it can be summed up simply: love them all, appreciate the service they're offering, and through it all keep your eye firmly on a goal—what must be accomplished.

Many churches have a form which lists all the avenues of work open to members of the congregation. If the church where you work doesn't have one, make up a sample form, check with the pastor, and initiate the program.

Keep your own list of people who have indicated a willingness to work in the church office. It is a good idea to keep a card file of all typists and of those who will answer the phone or who have other basic office skills. If there is no one in the congregation who knows how to operate the various machines in the church office, why not teach somebody?

The joy of your life will be the ones who are efficient, pleasant, and willing to help whenever needed. You will have no trouble with these people.

The bane of your life will be those who are willing to help, but don't know how and can't seem to learn (after they go home, you spend a lot of time undoing their mistakes). One church secretary was delighted when a member of the congregation called her and said, "I know how busy you are, and I'd like to help. What can I do?"

"Oh, manna from heaven!" thought the church secretary, but she was wrong. She put the lady to work addressing envelopes. The lady sat at the typewriter for several hours and finally handed the church secretary a couple of boxes of addressed envelopes.

The gratitude in the church secretary's heart soon turned to dismay. Either the name was spelled wrong, or the address or zip code was incorrect. The church secretary said nothing, took the envelopes home that night and corrected them, but from then on she was very careful to give her well-meaning volunteer jobs that she could handle.

Then there are the volunteers who say they'll help but don't show up. The church secretary learns very quickly which people are dependable and which ones are not. There will always be people who will feel an occasional flash of generosity and promise to help, but when the job needs doing, they don't show up to do it. If you get fooled by these people more than once, it's your own fault.

You may be asked to let someone work in the church office in order to gain some experience. An older woman perhaps, who wants to go back to work but needs to sharpen her skills and regain some of her confidence. Or a high school girl who wants to try her wings before applying for a "real" job. Help them, of course, but be smart and get some actual work done.

You will wish many times that there were no such things as volunteers. You will really rather do it yourself. But they are members of the congregation, and they are volunteering their services, and for the most part they mean well. You can't scold them or fire them. You can't even show your displeasure.

On the other hand, there are many times when you'll be very thankful for volunteers. One of those times is when you're set to go on a one- or two-week vacation. The church goes on, even though you're not there, and someone has to answer the phone, take care of the mail, and type the Sunday bulletins. You call your list and ask the volunteers how many days they can work, and in no time you have a volunteer force to cover for you.

A few churches hire someone to take over while the church secretary is on vacation, but most church secretaries have to handle this and call volunteers. You will, of course, maintain a file of names of people who have indicated a willingness to work in the church office. At least a month before your scheduled vacation, write to each of these.

Dear _____:
I will be away on vacation for two weeks beginning August 2. The church office will have to be covered in my absence, and I am again relying on your willingness to serve. Please write your name opposite the dates and times when you will be able to work and return to me before _____.

On a separate sheet of paper list the dates and times when the volunteers will be needed:

August 2: 9 A.M. to noon _____
1 P.M. to 5 P.M. _____

August 3: 9 A.M. to noon _____
1 P.M. to 5 P.M. _____

(list each day you will be away)

50

Your letter continues: (Or add this to the above schedule):

Your duties will be simple. Answer the phone; when the mail arrives, open it and distribute to the folders on my desk which are labeled, "for the minister," "financial," "bills." People will be stopping by for these folders.

If you find that you cannot come to work on your scheduled day, please arrange for someone to take your place or switch days with one of the other volunteers. Persons who are willing to be called in an emergency are:
(list names and phone numbers)

When you have received all the responses, type a vacation work schedule exactly like the one you sent with your requests for help, with dates and times, and include the names and phone numbers of the volunteers opposite the days and times when they will be working. Make sure that the minister and volunteers have a copy of this.

Of course, when you return from your vacation, you will remember to thank each of the volunteers. You might type a one-page letter thanking the volunteers and telling them how you spent your vacation. Duplicate this and send one to each. Be sure to keep a record of all this to use for next year's vacation.

Volunteers. The joy and the bane of a church secretary's existence. Treat them gently and kindly. Use them, but don't abuse them.

THE OFFICE ROUTINE

Right from the start, establish your first-of-the-morning routine. Believe me, it is important, because the phone will start ringing, people will be arriving, and away you go. I found it most convenient to arrive fifteen minutes early and do what I had to do to get ready for the day (if the phone rang before 9 A.M. I didn't feel guilty about letting it ring).

Some pastors are very well organized, but many are not. So you will want to start off on the right foot, establish the fact that you operate professionally, and know what you are doing.

The minister's office is almost always more than a place to work. This is where he receives the members of his congregation who come to him for many reasons. First

thing in the morning, check his office to be
sure it's neat, dust-free, and ready for him and
his visitors (or be sure the custodians do
this).

Priority Calendar

Every good secretary has one, but a church
secretary must keep a different kind of
calendar. Yours must be a priority calendar
that will be changed daily so be sure you have
a large one. These can be purchased or you
can make your own. At the beginning of the
week write in your own priorities. As the
minister and others come to you with
requests, for instance, a mimeographed program for the women's spring luncheon, or a
letter to church school teachers, ask them for
a date on which they must have this—the
latest date. Write the request on that latest
possible date.

Keep an indexed folder (or tickler file) of all
requests. As you do each task, strike it off
your calendar. It's important to keep this
calendar up to date because you will certainly
get many requests, and it's best to let
everyone know that they have to reckon with
your priority calendar.

Answering the Phone

Of course, you know how to answer the phone, but it's very important to do it right. To say, "Good morning, Redeemer Church, may I help you?" sets a nice tone and speaks well for the church. The phone may well be the bane of your existence. After all, there are fifteen hundred souls out there, plus innumerable other people, and they all find it very convenient to pick up the phone and call the church. No matter how many times you pick up that ringing phone, keep a pleasant tone in your voice. Be careful about taking messages for your boss, and be sure he gets them all as soon as you see him.

There will be many times when the pastor is in conference and absolutely cannot be disturbed. During these times it is almost a certainty that you will receive telephone calls from people who will insist on speaking to him. Of course, you're not going to interrupt the minister, so you must learn how to deal with this problem as effectively as possible.

It's a psychological thing you're dealing with. Everyone wants to feel that his minister is immediately available when needed. Probably some of them do have an urgent matter to discuss, some may feel a deep need to talk to him at that moment. Whatever the case, they are going to feel disappointment at being put off. You must assure them that their pastor will be concerned and will return their call the minute he is free to do so. You would, of course, list the calls in the order they came in, perhaps noting the time you received each call. However, if one of the callers mentions an emergency situation (a family member taken to the hospital, or other emergency), call this to the pastor's attention.

Handle as many of the phone calls as you possibly can. Get out of the habit of automatically ringing his phone everytime a caller asks to speak to the minister. Request the caller's name, and ask if you can be of any help. Nine times out of ten, you can. Many people call the church for information that you can easily supply. The minister is busy in his office, and he shouldn't be interrupted several times a day to tell people that Sunday services are at nine and ten A.M., or that the stewardship committee meets on Tuesdays. The more you free him from this sort of thing the more valuable you will be.

You will get many calls from church members asking for different kinds of information. The church school superintendent wants to know how many children were enrolled in the church school three years ago;

the president of the women's group has to know how many women have sent in reservations for the spring luncheon next week; a member of the youth group wants to know how many have signed up for the bowling team. Usually, these calls come when you're very busy. You would like to tell them to call someone else or to come in to the church office and look up the information themselves. However, remember public relations and be helpful. If you don't have the information at your fingertips promise to call back. I recall one day when I got so many requests for information my head was swimming. Somehow, I managed to look it all up and make the phone calls and get home in time for dinner. Later in the evening, as I stepped out of the shower, I remembered one phone call I had forgotten to make. I had looked up the information, however, and remembered it, so I made the phone call. That person was appreciative and told a lot of people about how thoughtful I was.

How you answer the phone, how you handle messages for the pastor, how helpful you are, are all extremely important. This is a big part of your job, and if you look on it as a means of good public relations and not as that monster that won't quit ringing, you'll be a much better church secretary.

Work-to-Be-Done Folder

In most secretarial jobs, when you leave the office on Friday you cover your typewriter, put away pencils, and leave your desk looking neat. When you return to your desk on Monday it's just as you left it. The church secretary leaves on Friday, and over the weekend a lot is going on in the church. When you return on Monday your desk will probably be covered with notes and requests from a lot of people. Make up a folder titled Work to Be Done and tell people to put their requests in that folder. This eliminates the possibility of some notes being lost in the shuffle. Some church secretaries are in their offices on Saturday and Sunday and have more control over this situation. Still, a work-to-be-done folder would be a great help.

THE SUNDAY BULLETIN

Typing the Sunday bulletin is one of the most important tasks a church secretary

57

performs. The bulletin is the church's calling card. Nothing less than perfection will do.

Some churches have an order of service that never varies (except for hymn numbers, scripture verses, and sermon titles). Others may change every Sunday. This will be dictated by the minister.

Be very sure of your spelling. If you're not absolutely positive about a word, look it up. A bulletin with misspelled words is not a good reflection on the church.

Keep left- and right-hand margins absolutely straight. As a typist, you know how to do this. Be extremely careful in the division of words. Again, when in doubt, look it up. In my early days as a church secretary, I was concentrating on keeping the right-hand margin straight, and I typed:

> The Reverend Doctor Blank of Peoria, therapist, will speak to the adult class next Sunday. This promises to be an exciting event.

Almost always on the back of the bulletin are the announcements, names of flower donors, and the like. The minister may determine what goes here. In any case, he will give the final approval, but it will probably be your job to receive the announcements and prepare this page in draft form for his approval. Here are a few things to consider:

Priorities

People will call you all week with items they want included in the back of the bulletin. Obviously, there will be many times when you will have more items than space. You can't say, "First come, first served". The notice of a meeting called for next week should take priority over a meeting scheduled for next month. Perhaps an item can wait for the next issue of the church newsletter.

General Interest

Most personal items (not of a wide, general interest) belong in the newsletter, not in the Sunday bulletin.

Coverage

Some items are intended for every member of the congregation. Not every member attends church services every Sunday, so this kind of item belongs in the newsletter which reaches everyone.

59

I wish that I could write a step-by-step procedure for typing Sunday bulletins. One that would be a model of efficiency and would work every time. Oh, how I wish I could. This book would then sell for at least fifty dollars a copy, and every church secretary in the country would buy one. I could attempt this, but church secretaries would only laugh. After all, it makes sense to state that you must have a deadline for bulletin items and that you must stick to that deadline. If there is a church secretary out there who has accomplished this feat, I must meet her.

The rest of us spend deadline day begging the minister for his sermon title, trying to locate the organist for the name of the prelude, and dealing with people who insist that their announcements have to go into the bulletin no matter what.

The best I can do is to suggest that you do set a deadline, try to get everyone to meet it, but don't lose your cool when it's not met. Just do the best that you can.

Keep a file of all the Sunday bulletins. For the records, for posterity. Keep them in the files, in folders. I would also suggest that you file one copy of each bulletin in a three-ring notebook and keep this notebook in the minister's office. He will find it very handy for reference. It is a simple task for you to punch holes in the bulletin and add it to the notebook every Friday. Sure beats having the pastor say, "How did we do that the last three Easter Sundays?" and your digging through the files to get copies of old Easter bulletins.

MEMBERSHIP LISTS

It goes without saying a church's membership lists must be kept current. Such lists will be changing constantly, and it is very easy to get behind. It is absolutely essential that you have a system.

If your system is to make the changes as they occur, it won't work. You're apt to receive a letter requesting a transfer to another church, a phone call giving you a change of address, notification by the pastor of a death, birth, or marriage all on a Friday morning when you're concentrating on the Sunday bulletin. So be sure to have a system and follow it.

There are several ways in which you can handle this.

1) Keep a notebook with the names of every member of the congregation in alphabetical order.

2) Keep a file drawer with a file folder for each family in the congregation. In the front of each folder keep a membership information sheet.

Assign each member family a number that corresponds to the number in the official church record book. These books can be purchased at a bookstore, and every church should have one. The pages are usually prenumbered and names are entered, with date of membership, as families join the church. There is space also for entering the date of death, transfer, or other termination of membership. Or

3) You can maintain an alphabetized 3 x 5 card file.

Remember that these records are confidential. They should be kept in a locked drawer or file cabinet. Of course, certain information, such as phone numbers or addresses, can usually be given on request, but items such as birth dates or facts of a divorce are confidential, and only you and the minister are to read these files.

When you receive notice of any change, jot the information on a piece of paper and put that paper into a special folder labeled Congregational Changes. Whenever you have some free time post those changes, or schedule a regular day and time for this task.

Getting the information for your membership lists is not always easy. We have the forms, we ask the people to complete them and give them back to us, and then we wait. We call, we beg, we plead, and still we wait. One way of beating this problem, if the minister gives his approval, would be to schedule a special meeting for the new members. This could be an informal meeting with the minister and his family, the church board, and perhaps committee chairpersons. At this meeting, which could be held immediately before or after the people join the church, the special needs of various committees, the program of the church, some facts the minister wants to convey would be discussed. Many churches do this, and if yours does, try to include completing the membership information sheets as part of that meeting.

It will not be your decision as to when to remove a name from the membership roster. Each church has its own rules concerning this.

It is also useful to keep little colored metal clips on hand. When a change comes through, put one of these clips onto the person's folder or card. This will remind you that there has been a change that has not been posted. When you do post the change, remove the clip.

However you decide to do it, remember that this is one of the most important tasks of the church secretary. If there are fifteen hundred members of the church, it is your responsibility to keep an accurate, up-to-date record of each of those fifteen hundred people. People move, die, get married, divorced, have children, and all these facts must be recorded. There will be times when several changes are thrown at you just when you are busiest, and there will also be times when you'll have to make phone calls, write letters, and ask around to find out whether or not a family has moved. In any case, it is important that you have a system.

There was probably some kind of system already in effect when you started your job. If it has worked, keep it. Perhaps you'll see ways in which it can be improved and made more efficient. You may want to initiate an entirely new system. If so, work up a sample, show it to the minister (he'll have some ideas and preferences), and when you have agreed on the system you're going to use, put it into effect and stick to it.

Membership Information

Family number:_____

Family Name: _____

Address: _____

Phone: _____

Business Address: (husband) _____

Phone: _____

Business Address: (wife) _____ Phone: _____

Husband: Date of birth:_____ Date of Baptism:_____

Date of joining church _____.

Wife: Date of birth:_____ Date of Baptism:_____

Date of joining church:_____

CHILDREN			
Name	Birth date	Date of Baptism	Date of Confirmation

Pertinent information:

THE CHURCH NEWSLETTER

Most churches publish a newsletter which is mailed to all members of the congregation and sometimes to friends of the congregation, former members, clerical friends of the minister, and other churches in the area. The newsletters can be weekly, bimonthly, or quarterly. Newsletters are the means by which the minister, members of committees, and others can relay information about the church, its members, and dates and times of meetings.

In all probability, there already will be a newsletter, and it will be your job to see that the information is gathered, compiled, edited, and published. Sometimes, a team of volunteers does this job, and the church secretary has nothing to do with the newsletter. If this is the case, you still may be able to offer some valuable advice to the volunteers to help them be more efficient and to put out a better newsletter. If there is no newsletter in the church where you work, why not start one? In any case, the following may help you.

First, a newsletter needs style, a certain look which identifies it. You can design a masthead and determine a name for the newsletter. You can have a year's supply printed if the church can afford this. If not, you will have to type the masthead on a stencil and run off a month's or a year's supply. Determine your style and stick to it. For example, the first page may contain "Notes from the minister." He knows that he is to write one page for each publication. On the second page you might always box a list of birthdays of the month. You may decide to have a one-page newsletter, or several pages in columns. However you do it, set a style and be consistent. Consider including a calendar of events in every issue. Also, instead of just typing paragraph after paragraph, try typing the pastor's message in letter form, the page of announcements in column form, and other news items straight across the page.

If the newsletter is small, one page, or is published only four times a year, you will be able to handle it with no help. However, a church that is large enough to hire a church secretary should publish a monthly newsletter at the very least, and if you are publishing a weekly or monthly newsletter, you'll need help, and that means volunteers.

In order to make the job go as smoothly as possible, act like a professional, know what you're doing, and make clear what you expect from each volunteer. Let's say you decide that a staff of five volunteers is exactly what you need to get the newsletter out each week or month. You secure the services of these five people, and the first thing you do is to make a schedule—with deadlines. Make sure that each volunteer has a well-defined job and a deadline to meet. You may have to help them find babysitters. You may have to make arrangements for some to work in the office in the evening when you're not there. There could be transportation problems. At your first meeting with the volunteer staff, try to recognize and iron out all these problems.

At the very least you will need persons for the following jobs (perhaps one person could handle more than one of these jobs):

- Typing the news items as they come in. These are to be typed (double-spaced) exactly as they are received. Later, you will need to do the necessary editing in preparation for a final typing.

- Selecting stencil illustrations for each issue.

- Cutting and pasting up the dummy.

(There may be more editing needed to fit the space available.)

- Cutting the stencils and running the newsletter, after the pastor's final approval of the dummy.

- Keeping the mailing list accurate and up-to-date.

- Addressing the newsletter. There are many ways to do this. Labels may be typed each month. A master set may be typed and xeroxed, as needed, or an Addressograph may be used. You might run several months of stenciled mailing lists and make corrections and changes later on for each issue. Try to find the fastest, most efficient method to fit your situation.

- Mailing. Depending on how many copies are to be sent, you will need several people to see to the actual posting. You will probably want to make this a bulk mailing, and it is necessary to have two hundred or more copies to qualify for this lower rate. (You will also apply at the post office for a bulk mail, religious, non-profit organization rate, which is even lower than bulk mail.) The post office has special rules and regulations on bulk mailing, especially for nonprofit organizations, so it's important that you actually go to the post office and get as much authoritative information as possible. Abide by the regulations, or you could lose the special bulk mail privilege.

Always keep to a regular publication date so that the members will know exactly when the newsletter will arrive. This will allow dates of meetings to be current.

Once you have received all the items for your newsletter, type them one after the other, in no particular order. Then cut out the separate items and paste them onto a dummy copy in the order and the arrangement you think best. Keep your priorities in mind. For example, you may have an interesting paragraph on some activity in a neighboring church. You feel that the members will be interested in this, and you plan to feature it across the top of page two. Then you receive a notice from a committee chairperson about an important, unscheduled meeting for the coming week. Of course, your interesting article must be replaced by the committee announcement. However, save the unused article for possible use in a later issue. Give the dummy paste-up to the minister for approval.

Determine a deadline for all contributions to the newsletter. In every issue, if possible, remind people of that deadline. All church secretaries have a lot of trouble getting people to meet the newsletter deadline. The newsletter is ready to run, and someone calls with an item that must be included. Or the church secretary tries every way she can think of to get news items with no success. She gives up, and puts some filler items in the newsletter. At the last minute, some congregational news items are brought in. How to solve this aggravating problem? Maybe the only way is to get tough, to say "I'm really sorry that I can't include your notice in the newsletter, but it came in past the deadline." It won't be easy to do this, but it might become necessary.

You should set up and maintain a production schedule. It would be a good idea to make this on a large piece of paper and perhaps hang it on the wall, so that not only you, but the volunteer staff (and the members) will be kept aware of deadlines to be met and duties to perform. This production schedule should be duplicated, and the appropriate names and dates filled for each issue of the newsletter.

71

Items for the newsletter will not be submitted to you in typed, double-spaced copy. Instead, you will receive scribbled messages on scraps of paper, articles read to you over the phone, recorded verbally on cassettes, you name it. Naturally, this is going to require some editing because you will want to submit a nearly perfect dummy copy to the minister for final approval. In your role as editor consider these points:

- Do you understand exactly what the writer is trying to say? If you don't, the reader won't either.
- Are the facts correct and in the right order?
- Is the statement made clearly with a minimum of words? (Don't be afraid to delete unnecessary words.)
- Check spelling, grammar, sentence construction.
- Check and recheck all dates, times, names.

As an editor, you must recognize the audience for which you are writing. The church newsletter is likely to be read by young and old. So, the newsletter must be simple enough for the young and interesting enough for older people.

Newspapers have long known the secret to writing for this audience. They use short, concise sentences and pack a lot of information into the short lead sentences of each article. You should try to do this. Give the "who, what, when, and where" in the first sentence of each article. Then, tell why. Use short sentences, and choose simple and effective words. Then you're bound to keep the young and old interested and reading.

Publishing the church newsletter could be the most enjoyable part of your job. It could also be the job you dread and despise. It's up to you to make it one that you enjoy, and the only way to do that is to be efficient. Know what you want to do, procure an efficient committee of volunteers, establish definite job guidelines, determine deadlines and stick to them. By the time you've published a couple of issues, you will probably discover that putting out the church newsletter is a lot of fun!

Good Tidings Newsletter Production Schedule			
ITEM	PERSON RESPONSIBLE	DATE TO BE COMPLETED	DATE COMPLETED
Type articles as they are received			
Cut and paste dummy			
Approve dummy			
Select illustrations			
Final typing			
Mailing list up-to-date			
Address newsletter			
Mail newsletter			

Calendar of Events • Grace Church • April 1979

1	2	3	4	5	6	7
Sunday Worship Services 9:00 AM 10:00 AM Sunday Church School 9:00 AM Adult Sunday Bible Class 9:00 AM				Women's Group luncheon 1	Missionary Group 2 PM	
8 Youth Group 6 PM	**9**	**10** Church Board 7 PM	**11**	**12** Maundy Thursday Worship Service 7:30 PM	**13** Good Friday Service 7:30 PM	**14** All-Church Workday 1-5 PM
15 Easter Sunday Breakfast 6 AM Service 8 AM Service 10 AM	**16** Nursery School Board Meeting 9 AM	**17**	**18** Morning Circle 9 AM	**19** Afternoon Circle 1 PM	**20** Evening Circle 7 PM	**21**
22	**23**	**24**	**25**	**26**	**27**	**28**
29	**30**					

GUEST PREACHER

When the minister is on vacation or ill or called out of town on an emergency, you may have to assist in securing the services of a guest preacher. The minister may ask a particular person, or he may give you several names in order of preference.

The minister may dictate a letter to you. He may call a clergyman and ask you to write a confirming letter. If he is called out of town suddenly or is taken ill, you may have to handle it all yourself. It would be a good idea to ask your pastor for a list of clergy and their addresses for your files in case you will be required to do this.

When you need the services of a guest preacher, call him first to determine whether or not he will be available on the Sunday you'll be needing him. Then write a follow-up letter.

Before writing the letter, determine how far the minister will have to travel. Will he drive? Fly? If he's going to fly, call the airlines for a schedule.

Perhaps it will be necessary for the guest preacher to stay overnight. In that case, you may need to secure a host family in the congregation who will be willing to house

him (another list you need to have on file).
Check with the church council or board to see
if the church will pay travel expenses, the
cost of a hotel or motel room if necessary, plus
an honorarium. Then write the letter.

If there is time, you will want to send an
announcement to the local papers. In your
phone call, request biographical data, sermon
title, and any other interesting information
from the guest preacher.

Before the minister leaves, ask him for his
expense account and arrange to give him a
check for that amount plus the agreed
honorarium. Try to avoid mailing him a
check later on. ·

If there are announcements that are to be
made from the pulpit on Sunday morning,
type them so that he can easily read them.

Sample Letter to a Guest Preacher

October 15, 1978
The Reverend John Blank
Grace Church
100 Main Street
Chicago, Illinois 60001

Dear Mr. Blank:

We are looking forward to having you with us on
Sunday, December 10. Our service begins at 10
A.M. and concludes at 11. I am enclosing

last Sunday's bulletin so that you may be familiar with our regular order of service.

I will need the following from you before Friday, December 8: hymn numbers for four hymns (processional, second hymn, pulpit hymn, and the recessional), scripture verses, and sermon title.

I have checked with Allway Airlines, and there are several departure and arrival times on Saturday, December 9: Arrival times: 3 P.M., 3:15 P.M., 3:30 P.M. and 4 P.M.. Departure times: 6 P.M., 6:20 P.M., and 7:45 P.M.. Please let me know your arrival time so that I can arrange for you to be met at the airport.

You indicated on the phone that you are willing to spend Saturday night with one of the members of our congregation. Mr. James Blankenship and his wife Jacqueline will be pleased to have you as their guest. They reside at 2102 Winchester Parkway (phone 312-233-4488), which is only three blocks from the church. They will bring you to the church on Sunday morning and will drive you to the airport in the evening for your return trip. You will be their guest for dinner also.

The church will pay for your airline tickets plus an honorarium of $100.00. I will see to it that a check is ready for you on Sunday before your departure.

Thank you very much for agreeing to help us during our minister's absence. If I can be of further assistance to you, please don't hesitate to call me.

Sincerely,

Jane Doe, Church Secretary

THE POLICIES AND PROCEDURE MANUAL

If the church where you work does not have a policies and procedure manual, it would be a very creative and helpful thing for you to initiate the production of one.

You can't do this job alone. After approval from the minister, secure the volunteer help you will need. This will be a long-range project, involving months of work, but when it's completed it will be invaluable.

The policies and procedure manual should be duplicated so that you, the minister, new employees, committee chairpersons, and officers of the congregation may have a copy.

This manual will be referred to on many

occasions: When the minister is out of town and not available to answer questions; when new employees are hired; and in many situations involving the congregation and the public.

Everything on which the church has established a policy or procedure will be included in this manual. If policies and procedures have not been spelled out, now is the time to get the proper people to do this.

Once you have started work, it will be your job to collect the items for inclusion. Lay out a few rules so that the job will go as smoothly as possible.

Steps to Take

Step one: Decide, with the minister, who will be responsible for editing the manual. The minister may want to do this himself, or he may recommend a capable person.

Step two: Go through the minutes in the church records, staff conferences, and so forth, and search out policies and procedures agreed or voted on in the past. Incorporate these in the manual. Some of them may need to be updated.

Step three: Ask staff members to contribute

all policies and procedures relating to their jobs.

Step four: Enlist the services of at least one person from each committee and organization in the church to submit all policies and procedures relating to their groups.

Step five: Be sure to ask all contributors, if at all possible, to type or print their contributions on an 8½ x 11 sheet of paper. This will make them much easier to alphabetize and sort.

Step six: Write out all policies and procedures for the church office and the church secretary.

Step seven: When all the items have been received, you (or someone appointed to this task) will have to rewrite each contribution so that the manual conforms to a general style. It should be written in the third person with a minimum of words. (If you request that it be written this way in the first place, that will cut down the amount of work later on.)

Step eight: Type a rough draft with an index or table of contents and submit it to the person who is editing the manual.

Step nine: When you receive the edited manuscript, retype the material in final form. (Consider beforehand how the manual will be bound; leave ample room for margins as you type.) Since the manual will, from time to time, require changes and additions, it would be well to consider having it in loose-leaf form.

Step ten: Once the manual is typed in final form and the sections are in proper sequence, give each item a separate number. Do not number the pages. The reason for this is that changes will be made, additions, and perhaps corrections, and you will only have to retype the page with the change. Also, by numbering only the items and not the pages you won't need to retype the index or table of contents unless or until a great many new items have been added.

Step eleven: The manual must now be duplicated and bound or put into notebooks. Type an attractive cover page. If the manual is to be xeroxed, it is simple job. If however, it is to be mimeographed, stencils must be cut, and so there is one more step to be taken.

Step twelve: As each stencil is cut, get someone to proofread it with you. One of you reads from the stencil while the other follows the final draft. This is an important step, so take your time and do it carefully.

A policies and procedure manual will differ in content with each church, but it will contain policies and procedures for some or all of the following:

Staff additions

Attendance at conferences and conventions by the clergy and the staff

Travel expense for staff and clergy

Insurance program for staff and clergy

Social Security program for staff and clergy

Church office hours

Paid holidays for staff

Termination of employment

Salary schedule for staff

Staff meetings

Paid vacations for staff and clergy

Job descriptions

Chart of staff organization

Chart of church organization

Sick leave policy for staff

Compensatory time or overtime pay policy

Use of office machines

Repair of building and equipment

Use of church and charge for outside groups

Use of church and fees charged for weddings and funerals for congregational members and for outsiders

Securing a supply pastor

Requests to use supplies and equipment

Lost and found items
Purchasing supplies and equipment
Stated hours of worship services
Admission of church members
Dismissal of church members
Handling of special offerings
Memorial funds
Insurance for buildings and equipment
Charter and bylaws
Roster of church officers
Roster of church organizations
Policies of church Sunday school

In other words, everything on which the church has established (or should establish) a definite policy or procedure is to be included in the manual.

A policy should be stated in a single sentence, if possible, followed by a definition of terms. Then a responsibility statement, concluding with a procedure for carrying out the policy. For example:

PURCHASES OF SUPPLIES AND EQUIPMENT: No puchases may be made and charged to the church without a purchase order number's having been issued. The church secretary, under the direction of the finance committee, will issue a puchase order number on request. When a question arises as to the amount of money to be spent, the church secretary will refer the question to the finance committee for a decision.

Each firm making a charge to an account of the church will be asked to show the purchase order number on its invoice.

When the policy and procedures manual is completed and distributed, you and the minister and the congregation will rest secure in the knowledge that:

1. all procedures and policies of the church have been thought out, and evaluated, and set down step by step;
2. the needed and necessary information is available in case of the absence of the minister or a staff member or in the case of need for orientation of a new minister or staff member;
3. the minister and/or office supervisor will be able to study the manual from time to time and determine whether or not all policies and procedures are being followed or if revisions are called for.

To give you an idea of how important a policies and procedure manual can be, in one church the church secretary was charging outsiders five dollars to use rooms and the kitchen in the church. When she started working for that church, she found a note taped to her desk: "No charge to members using the church and kitchen. Charge all outsiders five dollars." So the church secretary followed those instructions. Eventually, someone questioned this, calls were made to other churches to ask how much they charged, with the result that the fee was increased to twenty-five dollars. It was finally determined that the note taped to the desk was about fifteen years old. It was also estimated that the church had lost close to a thousand dollars.

RECORDS BOOK

Every church secretary soon discovers that files grow and grow. Periodically, it becomes necessary to clean them out, store them away, and start over. If an item in the files has not been used for several months perhaps it can be thrown away. If it is too important to be thrown away, but probably will not be used in the near future, it should be stored. These should be stored in boxes, in alphabetical order, in a safe, dry place in the church. I'm not advising you to throw stuff away, but if I found an outdated item that hadn't been used for at least a year, I'd toss it. However, use your own discretion.

A good idea is to initiate a Records Book. Simply list all the files in the church office in alphabetical order (leave spaces so that you can fill in the names of new files). At the right, indicate where that file is located. For example:

FILE	LOCATION
Annual Convention Notes 1975, 1976	Church basement
Annual Convention Notes 1977	Church office
Youth Retreat Information	Choir room cabinets

SUNDAY VISITORS

Each Monday check the visitor's book or the attendance record for names of visitors. In most cases, if a visitor writes his name he will also include his address.

Send each one a note, and at the same time make a list of the names and addresses on 3 x 5 cards and file with your prospectives. It would be a good idea to give a list to the chairperson of the evangelism committee.

Sample letter to local visitors:

Date
Name
Address

Dear _____:

We were pleased to have you worship with us on Sunday, June 6.

We hope that you will visit us again soon. If I can ever be of any assistance to you, please don't hesitate to call me.

Sincerely,
Raymond Jones, Minister
233-4466

For out-of-town visitors, change second paragraph to read:

The next time you are in our city, we hope that you will visit us again.

These may be handwritten, and you can sign the minister's name. Or perhaps he would rather have you type them on letterhead for his own signature. In any case, you assume the responsibility for getting the letters to the visitors.

BULLETIN BOARDS

Bulletin boards are marvelous things. They provide an attractive means of communication, a link between people and organizations within the church. Of course, they can be a real mess, too. All of us have seen the overflowing bulletin board in the hallway, with stale news, bits of paper tacked here and there. It's very easy to ignore.

Why not make the church office bulletin board your baby? Hang it in the place where the traffic is heaviest and keep it attractive, neat, and current. Set a certain day and time each week for updating the bulletin board. Mark it on your calendar. Remove all outdated items, and be sure only current information is posted.

- Check the local newspapers for items about church members.
- Post a list of all ill and hospitalized members with addresses so that friends can send cards.

Good Idea

89

- Post announcements of meetings.
- Post the current issue of the church's newsletter.

It would be a good idea to have a color-coded bulletin board. Once people become familiar with the code they'll appreciate it. Paste or staple certain items on a colored background. This could be:

- RED for important, urgent news
- GREEN for announcements of regularly scheduled meetings
- BLUE for lost and found items
- PINK for special events
- WHITE for all other items.

FORMS

Forms help get a job done. If a committee chairperson asks you to order supplies you could jot the information on a scrap of paper and later on locate the paper and order the supplies. This would probably work if you received very few such requests. But, as we all know, a church secretary receives numerous requests for services and supplies every day. Creating forms to help us in complying with these requests is an efficient way of doing the job. Following are a few things to consider:

- If multiple copies will be needed, consider a one-use carbon inserted in the form (fairly inexpensive ones with colored sheets of paper can be purchased).
- The form should be a size that is easy to handle and to file, and one that will not be easily misplaced.
- All forms should include the name and address of the church.
- When you design a form, be sure that blank spaces conform to the line spacing on your typewriter.
- A good idea is to use different colors of paper for different forms.
- File a copy of each form used in the church. Be sure a copy of each is included in the procedures manual. Write on each one a brief description of how it is used and when.

However, as efficient and helpful as forms are, we can become "form-happy," so there are some questions we need to ask ourselves periodically.

- Could some of the forms now in use be updated or changed or consolidated to be more effective?
- How frequently is the form used? Enough to justify its existence?

MAIL

- Stamp the date received on the back of each communication. Attach the envelope for possible reference.
- As you read each letter, note on the upper right-hand corner where it is to be eventually filed.
- If dates, times of meetings, and/or appointments are mentioned, jot these on your calendar immediately.
- If you note changes in addresses or phone numbers, write this information down for posting later to the proper record.
- Sort the mail for the minister. Place important communications on top, circulars, advertising, on the bottom

(much of the advertising you can file in your catalog file or throw away).
- If you frequently receive mail that requires a follow-up, it would be a good idea to keep a mail record.

Mail Record			
DATE	Description	to whom sent	Follow-Up Action to be taken
1/1/77	Letter from Dr. Smith	Mr. Jones	Set date for stewardship meeting
1/2/77	Letter from women's grp.	Mrs. Smith	Names of women who attended December meeting

When the action has been taken, simply draw a line through the item.

NOTES AND MINUTES

Some church secretaries attend meetings of committees and boards, take the minutes, and type and distribute them. Many get the minutes from secretaries of the committees and then type and distribute them.

Taking Notes

1. Take copious notes. It's better to have too many than not enough.
2. Record all specific motions, resolutions, amendments, and decisions verbatim with the full name of the person speaking.
3. Record the action to be taken. In the margin opposite these items, put a mark of some kind (an asterisk or an arrow). These will call your attention to the fact that these are items which require a follow-up by you or the minister.
4. Be sure to verify all facts and figures. Don't hesitate to ask, then and there, to have these repeated.

5. Whenever an important opinion is presented, enter it in the minutes exactly as it is given.
6. Transcribe the minutes into a rough draft as soon after the meeting as possible.

Typing the Minutes

1. Center, in caps, name of church, address, name of committee.
2. State time, place, and date of meeting.
3. Use 1½–½ inch margins.
4. Double-space between paragraphs.
5. Record what was accomplished, not what was talked about.
6. Record every motion, verbatim, whether or not it was carried.
7. Write out all sums of money with the figures in parentheses.
8. Indicate date of next meeting.
9. Note the time of adjournment.
10. Prepare a signature line for the presiding officer and include date of signing.

Keep a mailing list of all members of each committee and organization. Send agendas and copies of the minutes of them. Address envelopes ahead of time—either in your spare time or have volunteers do this.

Sample Minutes:

Grace Church
1001 Main Street
Chicago, Illinois

The Stewardship Committee

The Stewardship Committee of Grace Church met at the church on November 10, 1977, at 7 P.M.

Present: Jane Jones, chairperson, John Doe, Mary Smith, Bob Hill, Richard West

Absent: Gene Smith and Bob South

The Rev. John Jones opened the meeting with prayer.

John Smith moved that every member in the parish be called on between November 15, 1977 and December 15, 1977. After discussion, the motion was seconded and carried.

Bob Hill moved that subcommittees be appointed, under the direction of Mr. Jones, to accomplish this canvassing and visitation program. The motion was seconded and carried.

Jane Jones stated that she has talked to the church treasurer and that we will need pledges amounting to a total of three thousand dollars ($3,000) in order to meet next year's budget.

Mr. Jones recommended that the Stewardship Committee make an earnest effort to secure

pledges from all members of the congregation.
The next meeting of the Stewardship Committee will
be held on December 20, 1977, at 7 P.M. in the
church.
The meeting was adjourned at 8:15 P.M.

Respectfully submitted,

_____
Jane Jones, Chairperson
Stewardship Committee

RESOURCE FILE

It would be creative and helpful to initiate a
resource file for the use of the minister, the
director of Christian education, committee
chairpersons, heads of various organizations
within the church, and church school teachers. Once these people know that you are
maintaining a resource file, they'll be sure to
use it. Be certain that with the files you have a
large Out card. When persons remove any of
the files, they are to write their name and the
date they borrowed the file on the card and
place it in the file.

Some possible sources for gathering information for your resource file:

- The numerous publications the
  church receives

- Public library
- Magazines
- *Bartlett's Familiar Quotations*
- *Instant Quotation Dictionary*
- *Guinness Book of World Records*

Mark pertinent information. Paste the item on an 8½ x 11 sheet of paper. On top of the paper type the date, source, and page number. Determine the value of the material. If it's an item for the pastor, ask him to look it over before including it in the file.

File according to general subject interest. Keep on the alert for stories and articles that are short, to the point, and relevant.

ALTAR FLOWER CALENDARS

Altar flower calendars may be purchased at any religious bookstore. They are very inexpensive, and it would probably be wise to purchase one rather than to spend the time making one.

Usually, a member of the congregation

heads the altar flower committee and will
take care of the details. These include:

- Displaying the calendar in a promi-
  nent place so that members of the
  congregation can sign up.
- Arranging for publicity about the
  calendar through the Sunday bulletin,
  newsletter, and announcements.
- Following through after members have
  signed for specific dates. Calling to
  find out about desired dedications (In
  loving memory of _____; To the glory
  of God by _____; and the like) and
  passing this information to the church
  secretary for the Sunday bulletin.
- Sending out bills for the flowers and
  receiving the money to turn over to the
  church treasurer.

The church secretary must keep an accurate record of the donors. The head of the altar
flower committee should be instructed to give
you this list, along with the proper dedications, as far in advance as possible. You can
keep these in a small notebook or shorthand
pad for reference when typing the Sunday
bulletin. It is a good idea to save the lists you
receive in case any questions arise.

Be sure to check the spelling of names and
the exact wording of the dedications. One
church secretary was careless and the Sunday

bulletin announced that the altar flowers were dedicated by Mrs. Mary Smith in loving memory of her husband, Richard. Since Richard was very much alive, neither he nor Mary appreciated this error.

THE ANNUAL REPORT

In the church there are many committees, subcommittees, organizations, and departments. Reports from all of them will be included in an annual report. The annual report gives the history of the congregation for the year; what it has done, how it has been done, by whom, and how much it cost to do it. Also, the annual report records all membership changes during the year; the number of weddings, funerals, and baptisms; and how much money the congregation received and spent. It lists all staff members, directors, and chairpersons for the year.

As a church secretary, you will play an important role in collecting information and preparing and publishing the annual report. Do the very best job you can. Be creative, and make it attractive. The annual report could be merely a listing of facts and figures, one after the other, on one or two pages, but don't be satisfied with this kind of a report. Do your best. If necessary, during the last week or so of putting the report together, call volunteers to help in the office to free you so that you can concentrate on the report.

With the pastor, set a deadline for committee reports to reach you. Not everyone will meet that deadline, but if you set one, most people will at least try to meet it. Keep a checklist. As the deadline nears, get on the phone and remind the delinquent ones that you are waiting.

You will get reports scribbled in barely decipherable, penciled handwriting, recorded on cassette tape, jotted on scraps of paper, you name it. (One church secretary received some of the reports in line at the supermarket.) Your job is to put it all together into an attractive annual report.

Don't hesitate to do some editing. Check the facts, be sure they're correct, and rewrite sentences and paragraphs, if necessary, so that the report is as easy to read as possible. Be sure to check all spelling (especially names).

Even though you will receive items from many different sources, the annual report should have a consistent style. Except for the minister's report, rewrite each contribution so that all conform to one style. Check the annual reports of previous years to learn what style has been set. Try to be as consistent with this as possible.

Most annual reports are mimeographed and stapled together. It would be a good idea to make the cover from a colored sheet of paper, perhaps heavier than the rest of the report. Again, look through the reports of previous years. If your congregation is fortunate enough to have an artist, ask that person to draw a picture or design onto a stencil (can be done with a ballpoint pen) and use that for your cover.

Prepare a table of contents. Decide on a style (how much and when to indent, and so on), and stick to that style.

Be sure to include your report as church secretary. Keep it brief, to the point, and free of gripes. List your duties, some of the special things you've accomplished during the year, and perhaps a personal note on how you've enjoyed working with the minister and the people in the congregation.

Contents

Page

ANNUAL REPORT TO DENOMINATIONAL HEADQUARTERS

I can't tell you how to do this job, because this is laid out by your denominational headquarters, but this job can be made easier if you are well organized. One idea is to keep a notebook through the year so that when annual report time comes around, you will be ready with the facts and figures, instead of having to look them all up.

In the notebook label the sections Members Moved, Members Deceased, Members Dismissed, Marriages, Deaths, and so on.

List all the things that you will be required

Annual Report Checklist

Committee	Person Responsible	Report Submitted	Date of Reminder	Typed	Stencil Cut
Church Life	John Doe	7/4/77	—	7/6/77	7/15/77
Education	Jane Smith	7/2/77	—	7/4/77	7/15/77
Music/Worship	Ken Blank		7/9/77		
Minister's Report	Mr. Jones		7/9/77		
Director Christian Education	June Smith		7/9/77		
	Etc.				

to report on at the end of the year. As changes occur and events happen, jot them down, with names and dates, under the proper heading.

At annual report time it is a simple matter to type the report.

ORDERING SUPPLIES

Very few secretaries have to concern themselves with the ordering of supplies. Most business offices have a ready supply of paper, pencils, and paper clips. If a secretary needs additional supplies she asks someone for them or fills out a requisition. It's different in the church. In all probability, it will be your job to see that supplies are ordered and that there is enough on hand at all times.

If the church doesn't already have a system for ordering supplies, initiate one. Make up a request-for-supplies form. Be sure that everyone is instructed to fill out one of these forms and have it approved before you will order supplies. Check with the treasurer to be sure the proper account is charged and that there is enough money in that account.

Keep a running inventory. As supplies are received, used, and reordered, make a notation so that if someone asks you to order soap for the washrooms you will see at a glance that you have three cases of soap on hand and do not need to order any. You can also anticipate needs. If your inventory sheets show that you have one roll of white paper tablecloths on hand and you know that the women's association is planning a luncheon in three weeks, you can order more tablecloths.

You will have to check your inventory sheet against actual supplies on hand every six months or once a year. The only way you can do this is by taking a physical inventory. Schedule an inventory day with some maintenance personnel or a volunteer to help you, and get a volunteer to answer your phone during the hours you're taking the inventory. It will mean going into closets, storerooms, wherever the supplies are kept and counting them. If there are any large discrepancies between your inventory figures and the actual count, investigate.

You may prefer to keep a separate inventory sheet for office supplies, maintenance supplies, and kitchen supplies. In a small church this won't be necessary, but in a large church it would be advisable.

Make a purchase order form and use it to order all supplies, books, and equipment. Number the forms and file them by number as the orders are received. Number your purchase order forms by the year. For example, #78-1, 78-2, and so on. The next year, of course, they would be numbered 79-1, 79-2 and so on. Once the articles ordered have been received, jot down on the purchase order the date received. Then enter that item on your inventory sheet. Keep all of the purchase orders in a notebook in numerical order, and at the end of the year remove them, file them, and fill your notebook with new, numbered purchase order forms.

The account numbers are determined by the church treasurer. He will give an account number to each committee or organization in the church.

When the bill for the supplies comes in, and you have checked its accuracy, fill out a request for payment form and submit it to the treasurer for payment.

Request for Supplies

Date:_____

To:_____

From:_____
Request:_____

_____

_____

_____

_____

/s/_____
Approved:_____
Order date:_____
Purchase Order No.:_____
Account No.:_____

Purchase Order No._____

Grace Church
120 North Main Street
Lombard, Illinois 60521
Phone: 323-6577

To:_____   Ordered by:_____
    _____   Approved:_____
    _____   Account No._____

Date	Item	Unit Price	Total Amt.
Total			

Inventory

Office Supplies	On Hand 1/1/78	Used	On Hand	Purchased	On Hand
Paper—20 lb. reams					
Typewriter ribbon—black					
Housekeeping Supplies					
Liquid soap 8 oz bottles					
mop heads					
Detergent 12-oz. boxes					
Kitchen Supplies					
Paper tablecloths (white)—rolls					
Paper tablecloths (colored)—rolls					
Paper napkins (white)—pkg/100					
Paper coffee cups (white)—pkg/100					

Request for Payment

Date:_____
To:_____
From:_____
For: (Include purchase Order No.)

_____

_____

_____

_____

Amount Requested:_____

To:—————————————————————————————

_____

Account to be charged:_____
Approved:_____

PETTY CASH FUND

A petty cash fund is kept in the office for making small purchases such as stamps, gas for the lawn mower, and emergency office supplies.

The petty cash fund is not always the church secretary's responsibility, but if it is, there is a right way and a wrong way to handle it. If you do not have a petty cash fund in the church where you work, it would be a good idea to request one. The fund should be kept in the office safe, if you have one, or in a locked file or desk drawer. Be sure that you keep accurate records of its use.

Start the fund with a small, fixed amount. Remember that each expenditure requires a signed receipt and that the total of the receipts plus the remaining money in the petty cash envelope must equal the original amount of the fund.

In addition to the receipts, which are kept in the petty cash envelope, keep a petty cash record. Keep this in a small notebook.

When the fund needs to be replenished, submit a petty cash report to the treasurer.

112

Petty Cash Receipt Voucher

Number_____

Date:_____

Name:_____ Amount: $_____

For:_____

_____

_____

_____

_____

/s/ _____
          Payee

/s/ _____
      Received money

Petty Cash Record			
Voucher	Date	Amount	Purpose
#1	1/2/78	$2.50	Gas for lawn mower
#2	1/3/78	$1.50	Ten 15¢ postage stamps
#3	1/7/78	$6.50	Pastor took a guest to lunch
#4	1/9/78	$1.50	Emergency office supplies

Petty Cash Report

Date:_____
To: The Church Treasurer
Re: Request for $3.00

```
Balance brought forward 1/1/78              $4.00
    1/15/78   Sexton's supplies   $5.00
    1/16/78   Office supplies     $2.00
                                  ------
                                  $7.00
                                           $ 7.00
    Amount requested                       $ 3.00
```

EQUIPMENT INVENTORY

If the church doesn't have an equipment inventory it should. You can do one alone or with help from the custodians, or a team of volunteers can do it. Rooms can be divided among the various committees, with each committee responsible for taking an inventory of the contents of designated rooms. The committees should take the inventories on the same day because things like chairs and tables and pianos get moved from room to room at different times.

Once the initial inventory is accomplished, and you have gathered all the data, type the information, make copies for the minister and the chief lay officer of the congregation, and keep the original in your files.

ADMINISTRATIVE ASSISTANT

Sounds great, doesn't it? You've worked in this church as a secretary for two, three, four years. The congregation has grown, they've

115

Sample Inventory Sheet:

Item	Size	Color	Model Number	Brand	Purchase Price	Date of Purchase	Source of Supply
Mimeo-graph	Std.	Green	A466	IBM	$2,000	1/1/76	A.B. Dick Co., Chicago
Type-writer	Legal	Red	B661	IBM	$500.00	5/4/73	A.B. Dick Co., Chicago

hired an assistant minister, and both of you think it's time for you to move up.

The oft-repeated goal of this book is to elevate the position of church secretary/administrative assistant, so we don't want just the title. We want both of these titles to mean something—to us and to others.

If you're a mediocre church secretary, doing only the barest minimum, not particularly creative or careful, initiating nothing new, just being there from nine to five, you probably don't have the qualities needed to be an administrative assistant.

If you've been hard-working, creative in your approach, efficient in doing your job, able to relieve the minister of much of his office work, and proud of your job, you might be an excellent administrative assistant. Once you've received this promotion with its added responsibilities, the church will probably hire a secretary to assist you. Then you will have the opportunity to pass on your enthusiasm, your creative ideas, and your interest. You will be continuing in the process of making the specialized position of church secretary as rewarding as it is important.

It's important to discover whether or not you possess the abilities of an administrative assistant. If you do, you will go back to the first chapter of this book, and then get to

117

work. Believe that you'll make it! However, if you discover that there is one ability (or several) you don't possess, as you work at your job and go through this book, you can try to develop these skills so that when the position of administrative assistant is available (or created), you will be ready for it.

An administrative assistant has to be able to make important decisions, tell people what to do and how to do it, and generally tend to the business of the church. She must be able to do this on her own, leaving the pastor free for his many other activities. She will have dreams and plans and hopes, and she must know how to put them into action. It's an awesome responsibility.

LETTER OF APPLICATION, AND RESUME

You have worked as a church secretary for several years. Of course you love the job, but many things can happen to cause you to seek a similar position in another church.

Sometimes there's a change of ministers,

and, although you got along very well with your former boss, you and the new pastor find that your personalities clash. Perhaps your husband is transferred, and you go with him to another town.

Or, you've never worked as a church secretary, but after reading this manual you decide it's an exciting job and you want to try it.

Whatever your reason, you're looking for a job as church secretary, and you'll want to approach prospective employers in as efficient and professional a way as possible. So you'll need to write a letter of application and a resumé.

Here are some hints on writing a letter of application to accompany your resumé.

- Put the emphasis on the person receiving the letter, not on yourself.
- Be specific—don't waste words.
- Capture the reader's attention in the opening paragraph.
- Appeal to the needs of the recipient and show how you can meet those needs.
- Motivate the reader to some immediate action.

Here are some things to keep in mind as you write your resumé.

- Identify yourself by name, address, and phone number at the top of the page.
- Give a brief description of the job you're applying for.
- List your work experience, last job first, with dates of duration.
- Gives details of your educational background, and/or your on-the-job experience.
- Under the heading of special interests, list your hobbies, talents, community involvement.
- Do not include personal data such as birthdate, height, weight, marital status.
- Leave salary open. This will be negotiated during the first interview.
- Do not list references. Instead, offer to supply them on request.

(Sample letter of application)

TO WHOM IT MAY CONCERN:
(or to the minister)

I have visited your church on several occasions and have been amazed at the number of activities and programs your congregation participates in.

It is my feeling that you and your congregation would benefit from the services of an efficient

church secretary. I have worked in that capacity
for over five years, and I feel that I could fill the
position and save you time and work. I would
welcome the opportunity to discuss this with you.

I am enclosing my resumé for your consideration. I have resigned from my present position,
and my last day on the job will be November 10,
1977. It is essential that I start work in another
church as soon as possible after that date.

Thank you for your consideration.

Name
Address
Phone
Date

(A sample resumé)

Mrs. Jane Smith
1022 Main Street
Chicago, Illinois
Phone: 333-5566

I am applying for the position of church secretary
which involves, besides normal secretarial duties,
management of custodians, church library work,
and special research for sermon material.

My work experience is as follows:

Administrative Assistant
Grace Church
1222 South Street
Chicago, Illinois 60699
May, 1970—May, 1977

Church Secretary
St. Paul's Chuch
830 North Street
Chicago, Illinois 60688
June, 1965—May, 1970

Clerk-typist
Arco Company
1800 West Street
Chicago, Illinois 60655
June, 1962—June, 1965

My educational background is as follows:
Four years high school: Central High, Chicago
Two years college: Northwest University, Iowa

My special interests are:
Photography
Ice-skating
Reading
Member of local PTA
Active church member and church
school teacher

I will be happy to supply personal and business references upon request.

WHY NOT GET TOGETHER?

It would be a good idea to contact all the church secretaries in your area (in a large, metropolitan area this could run into the hundreds) and invite them to meet at the church where you work on a Saturday or Sunday afternoon for coffee and doughnuts, or make it a brown bag luncheon.

At that first meeting have on hand copies of all the forms you've designed, plus copies of the newsletter and bulletin. Share these with the other church secretaries.

Conduct a tour of the church office. Find out how many would be interested in meeting regularly (perhaps at the churches, maybe somewhere for lunch) to exchange ideas, problems, gripes, and happy things. One church secretary said to me, "I am talking to people all day long, and yet I think being a church secretary is a lonely job."

Getting together with other church secretaries would be a great morale booster. Arrange to hold these meetings at the various churches at first, so that you can take tours and get ideas firsthand.

Another great advantage in getting together with other church secretaries is that you can help each other. If your mimeograph machine breaks down and it's going to be several days before it's repaired, you can call another church secretary and ask to run your bulletins or newsletter on her machine. When you run out of supplies or need information or any number of things, you should be able to call on one another for help.

SUMMARY

You've read through the *Handbook for Church Secretaries.* Now what are you going to do?

It is my hope and prayer that you won't put it aside and never pick it up again. This book was written to be used. In most cases, you can use the forms and samples as they are, but you don't have to. You may want to change them to suit your particular situation. If so, do it!

There may be a paragraph here, or an idea there, that sparks your imagination and sets you to wondering "What if I . . . ?" If so, get going.

Church secretaries are in the enviable position of being able to be creative on the job, and my intention in writing this book was to ignite that spark of creativity, not to stifle it.

Now go through the book again, concentrating first on the items that particularly interest you. See the places where you can improve your working situation; or where you can be of more help to your boss; or where a certain job can be made easier or more enjoyable. Take the items one at a time. Concentrate on one until you've done everything you can with it. Then, go on to another one. It may take a long time, but eventually you'll find yourself doing your job more efficiently, pleasing your boss and the members of the congregation immensely, and deriving a lot of pleasure and satisfaction for yourself.

Finally, be happy with your job. Whether you regard it as a call from God or a nine-to-five job; whether you work full-time or only a day or two a week; whether you're paid a salary or work as a volunteer church secretary, you can be happy and take pleasure in your work. Remember, for every person who complains, there's another one who brings you a plate of home-baked cookies. And for everyone who gives you too much work to do, there's another one who takes you to lunch.

Through my correspondence with church secretaries all over the United States I have discovered that many are much too busy, hate that ever-ringing telephone, are often frustrated, confused, and just plain angry. However, one fact stands out: nearly every church secretary says that she loves her job and is happy doing what she's doing.

I wish you luck and God's blessings!

INDEX